D1355297

REX CONWAY'S
GWR
ALBUM

The History Press

First published 2009

The History Press
The Mill, Brimscombe Port
Stroud, Gloucestershire, GL5 2QG
www.thehistorypress.co.uk

British Library Cataloguing in Publication Data.
A catalogue record for this book is available from the British Library.

ISBN 978 0 7524 5153 4

Typesetting and origination by The History Press
Printed in Great Britain

Contents

GWR 'Barnum' no. 3224 near Slough.

De Glenn Compound GWR no. 103 ready to leave Paddington with a train for Oxford.

Introduction

Once again looking through my archive, I realised how many Great Western Railway loco images I have in my collection. On closer examination I found that there are areas that are well represented, such as Old Oak Common and Swindon. Other locations are neglected, owing to the fact that photography was expensive and travel by car was solely for the well-off. Most photographers only recorded their own area, or possibly took some shots on their annual holiday. A great many negatives in my archive are glass, taken on large cameras mounted on tripods; the quality is superb, taken by real photographers, not like today's cameras where the person pressing the button does not need to know anything about photography, focus or exposures; dozens of pictures can be taken within seconds and prints can be made as quickly. Having been a professional photographer for over fifty years I have great admiration for those early photographers. I hope my selection will be of interest to readers and, as with my other books, I appeal to anyone who spots any incorrect information to contact me via the publishers. Any archive is reliant on information that comes with the negative and sadly this is not always accurate or, worse still, it comes with no information at all. I hope you enjoy the book.

Rex Conway, 2009

0–6–0 pannier tank GWR no. 323 with its driver posing for the camera.

Rex Conway's GWR Album

Richard Trevithick, acknowledged as the inventor of the moving steam engine, was ahead of his time. The materials and tools were not as advanced as his designs and vision. He built his steam engine and ran it on cast iron rails, the strongest material available in the early 1800s. However, cast iron is brittle, with the result that rails were constantly breaking, and a loco was likely to be derailed. A decade on wrought iron was developed, changing the viability of the moving steam engine. Such names as Stephenson (George and his son Robert), and Timothy Hackworth were building engines for working in collieries in the north conveying coal to canals and harbours, freeing hundreds of horses to take retirement. Then came the opening of the first proper railway – the Stockton & Darlington in 1825. All this had not gone unnoticed by the Bristol Merchant Venturers. Legend has it that some of the merchants met in a local hostelry in Bristol. One can imagine oil lamps smoking and sawdust on the floor. These gentlemen sat around a table in their tall hats with pints of the local brew in front of them, the conversation all about the events up north; 'Why can't we have a railway from Bristol to London?' Interest is aroused and, being merchants, pounds, shillings and pence become the major topic; how much could they save? How much could they make? Not having pocket calculators I have no doubt the table quickly became covered in scraps of paper with jottings and calculations. They must have arrived at a figure that would make them even richer as a railway was proposed, and the bill passed through parliament in 1835. Then came the appointment of an engineer. It is well-documented that Isambard Kingdom Brunel got the job. In 1833, aged only twenty-six, he had to survey the route, negotiate with landowners and oversee virtually every aspect of building a railway. He had a specially built coach, drawn by fast horses, which he frequently slept in. Surveying done, route selected, he just had to build the railway, dig a few tunnels, throw up a few bridges, the odd embankment or two and, oh yes, a few stations to design as well! The railway building started at both ends at the same time; Bristol and Bishop Road (Paddington). Brunel's original station in Bristol, a terminus, was built at right angles to the Bristol & Exeter (B&E) station with a curving line passing both stations. This line was for express trains between London and the west. Bristol was once a stronghold of the Knights Templar. There are many old streets named after the Templars, including one that leads to the station in Temple Way – hence the name Temple Meads.

The Bristol & Exeter Railway Terminus, which was built in 1845, was at right angles to Brunel's GWR station. It was a wooden shed and not very attractive when compared with the B&E offices, shown in the picture below. Bristol Temple Meads is seen to the right, while Brunel's GWR station can just be seen in the background to the left. It was an impossible situation as trains could not run through, so a connecting curve was built. As Brunel was engineer to the Bristol & Exeter as well as the GWR, I have no doubt he convinced the boards of both railways that a new station should be built on the curve. This was done after his death, during the years between 1865 and 1876. Apart from platform alterations in the 1930s, the Temple Meads of today was born. The aerial view at the bottom of the page shows clearly both the GWR and B&E Buildings and the present Temple Meads built on the curve.

The Bristol & Exeter offices.

An aerial view of Bristol TempleMeads.

Bristol Temple Meads opened to traffic in 1841, and the first train was to Bath, headed by 'Firefly' Class 2–2–2 *Fireball*. As traffic increased, it became obvious by the 1860s something had to be done. A new station built on the curve of the express line came into being in 1876. At the same time the Bristol & Exeter Railway amalgamated with the Great Western Railway. The Midland Railway used the original Brunel train shed while the GWR used the curved station. There were more alterations in 1935 when an island platform was removed and a subway added. The passenger bridge over the tracks was taken down as well. It was also decided to modernise the signals, and colour light signals, and the two new power signal-boxes were introduced; that's how Temple Meads remained until the 1970s. In 1844, the line from Bristol to Exeter was completed, and to mark the occasion a special train of invited guests travelled from Paddington through to Exeter, 194 miles non-stop, except for watering. What a photograph it would have made; it was headed by a 'Firefly' 2–2–2 and driven by Gooch himself. He completed the journey in five hours. The Great Western Railway was built to broad gauge – 7ft at Brunel's instigation. There is no doubt it was a safer and faster track, but all other railways were being built to the narrow gauge, 4ft 8½ins. This was the gauge that George Stephenson built in the north, based on his years of experience in the coal mines where the wagon ways were built to this width so that horses could walk easily between the rails. The Gauge Commission, which sat in judgement in 1845, favoured the standard gauge, not on safety or speed, but on interchange, and that there were many more standard lines than broad. You can imagine the frustrations of passengers or goods carriers arriving at Bristol Temple Meads on the Midland line, wanting to continue to Exeter by the GWR, having to unload luggage and mountains of goods. Brunel had proved that his broad gauge was safe and fast. In the late 1840s, trains were running in excess of 70mph but he thought that all other railways would follow the GWR once its success was proven; regrettably, they did not.

Rebuilding Temple Meads in 1936.

The Bristol & Exeter Railway, with its 9ft single locomotives, began running trains from Bristol to Bridgwater just before Temple Meads opened to traffic in 1841. It would be 1849 before the line was complete to Plymouth, and another ten years before Truro was reached. It was on the stretch of line between Bristol and Exeter that, in 1904, *City of Truro* came hurtling down Wellington Bank and broke the 100mph, something like breaking the sound barrier in a jet aircraft. *City of Truro* was at the head of an 'Ocean Mail Special'. The train was waiting at Plymouth Mill Bay for the mail from *Kronprinz Wilhelm* which had come from New York and arrived in Plymouth early morning on 9 May 1904. Nearly 1,400 bags of mail were loaded aboard the train and *City of Truro* was off. It was a record-breaking run to Bristol, where the *City of Truro* came off the train and no. 3605 *Duke of Connaught* continued the high-speed run to Paddington. Arriving early, it had covered the 118 miles from Bristol in 99 minutes, (not much longer than today's HST), travelling in places at 90mph.

With the coming of the railways, something else had to change; time. It was impossible to compile a timetable owing to differences in time between London and the rest of Britain. The only way was to adopt Greenwich Mean Time, and a daily ritual using the newly invented telegraph was enacted at Paddington, telegraphing London time to all parts of the GWR. The difference at Temple Meads was ten minutes; there is still a clock on the Exchange in Bristol that has two minute hands with ten minutes' difference.

Exeter St David's station in the 1930s.

Leaving Bristol, the London route to Bath was completed and opened for traffic in 1840. On this short route of about 12 miles, Brunel had to build a number of tunnels. Shortly after leaving Bristol comes the tunnels at St Anns and then the well known Fox's Wood Tunnel. Over 1,000 yards long, it is turreted at the western end, but Brunel left the eastern end as natural rock. Later on, troughs were laid here, drawing water from the nearby River Avon. A few miles on comes Twerton Tunnel and then it's into the Georgian City of Bath and Bath Spa station. Having left the station it's Sydney Gardens next, another dream-like location for railway photographers where you can sit on a grassy bank with its beautiful trees, squirrels scurrying around looking for nuts, with a low balustrade wall at the side of the railway and lovely wrought iron bridges for pedestrian use. I know what's in my mind when I sit there, visions of 2-2-2 'Fireflies' with their long chimneys, and later *The Great Bear*. We can all dream! On to Chippenham and then Swindon; to a GWR enthusiast, this is next to heaven.

Regarding the early locomotives for the GWR, these were built by outside contractors including the Stephensons. Brunel himself tried designing engines. He may have been a brilliant engineer and designer but steam engines seemed to cause him problems, as they were mainly underpowered. Realising he could not do everything, and being man enough to admit it, it was decided to appoint a locomotive superintendent. A young man, who learnt his engineering skills with the Stephensons at their locomotive factory in Newcastle and who had also worked on the Manchester–Leeds Railway, was informed that Brunel of the Great Western was looking for a superintendent. He applied and Brunel appointed Daniel Gooch to this senior position; he was not yet twenty-one! When he arrived to take up his post, he quickly realised that the locomotive stock left a lot to be desired. He immediately set about designing more powerful engines, including 8ft singles built to the broad gauge. So successful were they that speeds approaching 60mph were attained. Within a couple of years of completion of the line between Bristol and London, it was decided a locomotive works was required. Brunel and Gooch looked at a number of sites, but eventually standing in a field near a little village called Swindon, Brunel turned to Gooch, (and here I can only guess what was said). 'Well what do you think, Dan?' 'I think it's just what we want, Mr Brunel. Why, it's nearly flat all the way to London and there's the junction to Gloucester. It could not be better.' By 1843 the works had been built and in 1846 the first engine rolled out, it was 2-2-2 *Great Western*. Numbers were not used in the early days of the GWR; all engines were recognised by names. Gooch continued to look after the locomotive needs of the Great Western Railway until 1864, when he resigned his position to look after his business interests. He was persuaded to come back to the GWR a year later as chairman. His position as locomotive superintendent was taken by Joseph Armstrong until 1877, followed by William Dean until 1902 when Churchward took over. Creating a long line of highly successful 4-6-0s, starting with the 'Saints', he named the first one *William Dean* after his old boss. The 'Saints' were followed by the 'Stars'. Numerous other Classes were credited to Churchward including the first British Pacific 4-6-2 *The Great Bear*. Also he bought three De Glenn Compounds from the French for trials on the GWR to see if they were better than his 4-6-0s. The result was that the 4-6-0s won. Churchward retired on 31 December 1921 and was succeeded by C.B. Collett.

Churchward was a little hard of hearing and one fateful day in 1933 an autumn mist was swirling around the railway tracks. Although retired, he still lived in a company house called Newburn House which was close to the tracks, and he enjoyed a short walk from his home to the works most days. But that day in 1933, he made a fatal mistake of crossing the track as an express was approaching. He was run down and killed by no. 4085 *Berkeley Castle*. Swindon Works and the town were devastated; Churchward was immensely popular with the GWR workforce and the people of Swindon and thousands lined the route of his funeral procession.

No. 4085 *Berkeley Castle* arriving at Bristol Temple Meads.

North Star, built by Robert Stephenson at their Newcastle Works in 1837, was originally destined for the New Orleans Railway, but the order was cancelled and the engine was acquired by the Great Western Railway. It arrived by barge at Maidenhead on 28 November 1837. In fact, it arrived six months before the railway was built. When the rails finally arrived, it worked the first Great Western passenger train, which was a director's special. It was a very reliable engine, its unladen weight was nearly 25 tons. There were a further eleven of the 'Star' class, built between 1837 and 1841. In the 1850s *North Star* was rebuilt with a domeless boiler and ended its working life in 1871, when it was put in store in Swindon Works. In 1906, Churchward, on one of his many tours of the works, decided that it was taking up space, and ordered its destruction; a very sorry decision. A full-size replica was built at Swindon in 1925 and it is this replica that could be seen on a pedestal in Swindon A Shop.

North Star in Swindon Works.

The first locomotive built entirely at Swindon, and designed by Gooch, was a 2–2–2 with 8ft driving wheels and was appropriately called *Great Western*. It reached speeds of 60mph regularly. Regrettably it was scrapped in 1870. Another old GWR engine awaiting scrapping is this view of 'Barnum' 2–4–0 no. 3225. Built in 1889, it is awaiting the torch on Swindon dump in September 1935.

There were several crane locos built at Swindon especially for use at Swindon Works. This view is of no. 18 *Steropes*, built in 1901.

A general view of the works yard showing pannier tanks, 'Castles' and various other classes.

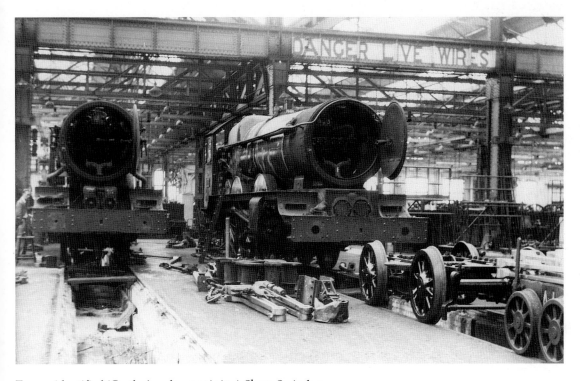

Two unidentified 'Castles' under repair in A Shop, Swindon.

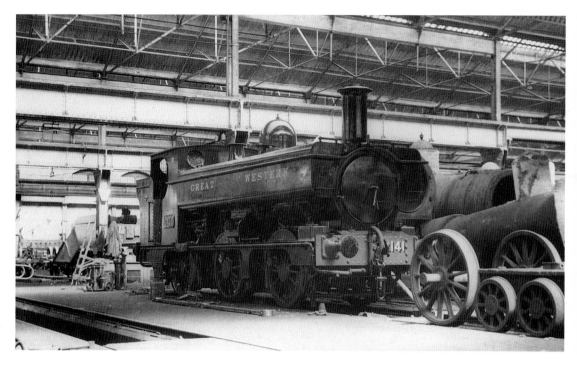

No. 2141 0–6–0PT introduced by Dean in 1897 as a saddle tank and later rebuilt as a pannier tank.

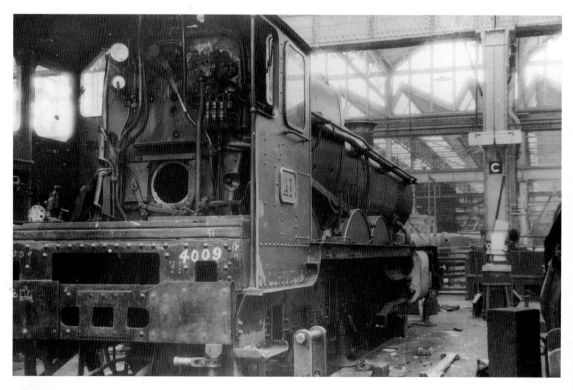

'Castle' class 100 A1 *Lloyds*. This loco was originally 'Star' no. 4009 *Shooting Star*, built in 1907. It was rebuilt as a 'Castle' during the late 1920s. It received the name *Lloyds* in 1936, named after the famous insurance company. It was taken out of service in 1950. This view is in Swindon A Shop in 1938.

GWR 'Bulldog' no. 3300 photographed at Swindon in November 1935. It was withdrawn in January 1936. Originally built as a 'Duke' in May 1895, it was withdrawn from service in November 1908 and re-emerged from Swindon Works as 'Bulldog' no. 3300 *Pendennis Castle* a few months later. The name was removed in 1923 and transferred to 'Castle' no. 4079.

0–6–0 PT no. 1366 introduced in 1934 by Collett, based on an earlier class designed and introduced by Churchward in 1910 for dock shunting. This view is on Swindon Shed in 1936.

'Aberdare' no. 2613 at Swindon in 1935, built in 1903 and withdrawn in October 1938. Their nickname 'Aberdares', came from the traffic they worked; heavy coal trains from the Welsh coalmines, to the fires of the south and west, for domestic and industrial use as well as the fireboxes of the GWR. The 'Aberdares' owed their life to the 'Kruger' class built between 1899 and 1903. These locos were rather ugly-looking machines, and not very successful. They only survived a short while and were taken out of service after only very low mileages, (30,000–70,000). However, valuable experience had been gained, and the more successful 'Aberdares' were born. In fact several survived into British Rail, being withdrawn in 1949.

GWR pannier tank no. 1179. Originally built as a broad gauge 0–6–0 saddle tank, it was converted in the 1890s to standard gauge. This view is in C Shop, Swindon, in 1935.

GWR nos 7, 8, 14, 16; these locos were originally 2–4–0s. Nos 7 and 8 were Compounds; 14 and 16 Simple and all but no. 7 were broad gauge convertibles, rebuilt to standard gauge in 1894. They were rebuilt again to a 4–4–0 with taper boiler in the 1900s. The first to be rebuilt was no. 16 *Brunel* in September 1901. No. 7 *Armstrong* was next in 1905 followed by no. 14 *Charles Saunders* in 1909. The last to be rebuilt was no. 8 *Gooch* in 1911. There were various other changes in their life, including renumbering when they became 4169 to 4172. In the early years they were used mainly on the London–Bristol route. In about 1910 they were transferred to the Wolverhampton division where they ended their days on local trains and station pilots. All were withdrawn by 1930.

'Armstrong' 4–4–0 photographed at Oxford in 1903. Loco no. 14 was named *Charles Saunders* after the superintendent of the line who also held the post of General Manager of the GWR. Saunders retired in 1863 after thirty years of virtually managing the affairs of the GWR single-handedly.

'Armstrong' 7ft no. 7 *Armstrong*, originally named *Charles Saunders* for a short time, but that name was transferred to no. 14. Joseph Armstrong succeeded Gooch as locomotive superintendent of the GWR at Swindon in 1864. Newburn House was built for the Armstrong family, and has been home for all the locomotive superintendents as it was only a short distance from the works.

No. 14 *Charles Saunders* with five cleaning lads posing for the camera.

'Dean Single' 4–2–2 no. 3056 *Wilkinson* photographed at Oxford in 1902. When built in March 1895, it was given the name *Timour* but was renamed *Wilkinson* in July 1901. Joseph Wilkinson was appointed general manager of the GWR in 1896. He was a brilliant manager who was knighted for his services to the GWR and had the final accolade of having a locomotive named after him.

The 'Dukes' were introduced in 1895 by Dean to work the steep banks of Devon and Cornwall. The first of the class was named *Duke of Cornwall*. However, the nameplate did not suit the engine; it was straight and mounted on the side of the boiler. This design did not last long, and the traditional GWR curved plates were fitted by 1903. They had small wheels, only 5ft 7in, but were powerful and very capable of handling the trains at the turn of the century. Their tenders were a bit on the small side, with only a capacity for 2,000 gallons of water. They were very efficient and well-loved by their drivers. The first to be withdrawn was no. 3263 in 1936, but a few lasted into British Rail days. They worked all the expresses from Exeter to Penzance, but gradually disappeared as the bigger 4–4–0s 'Bulldogs', 'Counties', 'Cities' and the 2–6–0 Moguls of the 43xx, came into traffic and trains got heavier. By the 1920s there were only a few left in the West Country and they were either working branch lines or used as bankers. The majority of the class were transferred to Didcot, Reading, Bristol and Shrewsbury, with the odd one or two transferred to other sheds. Didcot had a number and these were used on the Midland & South Western Junction Railway (M&SWJ) line to Southampton. Gradually the Cambrian line was allocated a large number which is where the final survivors saw out their duties; *St. Austell* was the last survivor, being withdrawn in 1951.

'Duke' no. 3278 *Trefusis.*

'Duke' no. 3257 *King Arthur.* A number of this class were named after characters and places in the Arthurian legend of the West Country. The name *King Arthur* was removed in 1927 when the 4–6–0 'King' class took to the rails. This photograph was taken in 1930.

4–4–0 'Duke' no. 3267 *Cornishman* here viewed on Didcot Shed in September 1934. Built in November 1896, it was withdrawn after forty years' service in 1936 having completed over one million miles!

'Duke' no. 3270 *Earl of Devon* photographed at Old Oak Common in 1912. The engine lost its nameplate in 1936 to the new 'Dukes' that were built in that year, and were named 'Earls', which in turn lost the earl names to the new 'Castle' class.

No. 3279 *Torbay* built in March 1897. Its original number was 3290. It is photographed here about to leave Teignmouth in the late 1920s. It was withdrawn in 1938.

'Duke' class 4–4–0 no. 3266 *Amyas*. Originally, when built in 1896, it was no. 3272. Most of the 'Duke' names can be easily traced, but *Amyas* has beaten me. Perhaps a reader knows, and could let me know? This photograph was taken at Didcot in the 1930s.

'Duke' no. 3285 *Katerfelto* ready for duty at Reading in 1933.

GWR 4–4–0- no. 3304 *Oxford* built originally as a 'Duke' in 1896. It was rebuilt as a 'Bulldog' before 1909, but by then its name had changed to *River Tamar*. It is photographed here around the turn of the century in Oxford.

Appropriately photographed in the West Country, 'Duke' no. 3264 *Trevithick* is named after the Cornish inventor of the first moving steam engine.

When built in January 1897, this 'Duke' was numbered 3278, and was named *Eddystone* after the lighthouse of that name. It is photographed on a rainy day at Borth, halfway between Dovey Junction and Aberystwyth on the Cambrian line.

'Duke' no. 3272 *Fowey*, named after the Cornish fishing port made famous by the novels of Daphne Du Maurier. The locomotive lost its name in 1930 at the request of the GWR traffic department, who received complaints from passengers because they thought it was the destination of the train. Many other engines lost their names for the same reason. One has to wonder at the common sense of these complainants!

This loco could be a 'Duke' or a 'Bulldog'; it has the cab and other fittings of a 'Duke' but the frames and wheels of a 'Bulldog' with engines that were taken out of service, rebuilt in 1936, and called 'Earls'. To me they are 'Dukes' in all but name. Speaking of names, many of the human earls thought it was a bit of an insult to put their titles to such an old-fashioned locomotive, and demanded their names should adorn the new 'Castle' class engines. Egos were satisfied when this was done. This view is of no. 3203 *Earl Cawdor*.

'Duke' no. 3281 *Cotswold* photographed at Paddington in the 1920s. Originally no. 3313, it was built in 1899 and scrapped in 1937.

The 4–4–2 tanks replaced the '3600' class on the Paddington suburban services to Reading and beyond, with 6ft 8in wheels and nearly 200lb boiler pressure. Their acceleration and higher running speeds made them ideal for local work out of Paddington. Built in the early part of the twentieth century, they did not have a long life; most were scrapped by 1934. They were displaced by the '6100' class of 2–6–2 tanks. The whole class of thirty engines was fitted with two-way water pick-up apparatus, but this was removed from 1921 onwards. In 1909 no. 2225 was painted crimson and worked the Bristol area. Another experiment in paint in 1920 was no. 2241 which was painted in a sand colour. Most of the class were fitted with audible cab signalling apparatus, some as early as 1908.

'County' tank 4–4–2T no. 2236 photographed at Paddington in about 1919, showing clearly the semi-circular vents on the side tanks and also showing that water pick-up apparatus was still fitted.

'County' tank no. 2221 at Reading in 1930. This was the first of the class, built in 1905, withdrawn in 1933.

4–4–2T no. 2224 photographed at Didcot in about 1924, a little off its usual area. Some of the class were tried in other areas, such as Devon and the Wolverhampton routes, but they were not popular.

GWR 'County' tank no. 2243 on a suburban train at Reading. This loco, built in 1912, was withdrawn in 1934 but survived as a stationary boiler at Old Oak Common before finally meeting its end at Swindon in 1939.

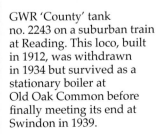

The 0–6–0 saddle tank was very popular in the early days of the GWR. They were built in their hundreds and could be found all over the system. They were gradually rebuilt into pannier tanks, although there were still a number left in the 1930s.

Burry Port & Gwendraeth Valley Railway (BP&GVR) no. 2195 *Cwm Mawr* photographed on Weymouth Quay in 1934. Built for the BP&GVR in 1905 by the Avonside Engine Co., Bristol, which was absorbed by the GWR in 1923, it went to Swindon for a GWR boiler to be fitted. Also, the coal bunkers were extended. The loco returned to traffic in 1926, and was sent to Weymouth, staying there until 1939, when it left for Bristol where it spent its last days.

GWR saddle tank no. 2020 with brass dome and copper-capped chimney. Here it is posed for the camera in Plymouth in the 1920s.

Llanelly & Mynydd Mawr Railway (L&MM), no. 359 *Hilda*, built in 1917 by Hudswell Clarke. In 1924 it started work in Swansea Docks, where it worked until it was withdrawn in 1954. It was the only L&MM loco to keep its nameplate. This photograph was taken at Danygraig in 1930.

Burry Port & Gwendraeth Valley Railway, no. 2196 *Gwendraeth*. This was no. 6 on the BP&GVR stock list and was built in 1906 by the Avonside Engine Co., Bristol. With a smashed window, it's looking a bit sorry for itself in this view at Danygraig in 1932. It was withdrawn in 1956.

GWR 0–6–0 saddle tank no. 1331, photographed at Swindon in 1935. It was rebuilt and returned to stock in 1926.

GWR no. 2118 0–6–0 saddle tank shunting at Looe in 1923. The crew seem relaxed and pose for the camera.

This 0–6–0 saddle tank had a long life. Built in 1865 for the Mawddy Railway, it was taken over by the Cambrian Railway in 1911 and then by the GWR, when it received the number 824. It was built by Manning Wardle and lasted until 1940. This picture was taken at Oswestry in the 1930s.

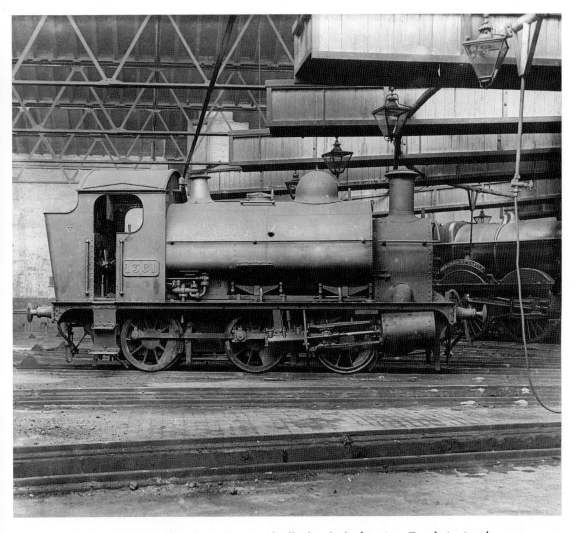

GWR 0–6–0ST no. 1361 introduced in 1910 specifically for dock shunting. For their size they were very powerful. With a short wheelbase and a weight of 35 tons, they could negotiate the dock lines easily. No. 1361 was photographed in Plymouth Laira shed in the 1930s.

Below are two 0–6–0 pannier tank locos that saw service in the suburbs of London, particularly the Metropolitan lines to Smithfield Market. They were fitted with condensing gear and a large pipe that took the exhaust smoke and steam (which normally went up the chimney) back into the water panniers, thus enabling them to work through the Metropolitan tunnels without gassing the crew. One drawback was that after quite a short time, the water in the panniers started to boil with the result that the engine had to be rested until the water cooled.

0–6–0PT GWR no. 8700, posed in Old Oak Common yard, 1934.

GWR no. 9710 in Old Oak Common, 1935.

GWR 0–6–0 pannier tank no. 1263, built in 1877 as a broad gauge saddle tank. Here it is photographed at Didcot with a spark-arresting chimney for working the nearby Ordnance Depot, 1935.

Arriving at Ealing Broadway with a one-coach train is 0–6–0PT no. 5412 in 1936.

Nos 102, 103 and 104 were known to railwaymen as Frenchmen. Churchward was interested by these locos when he saw similar engines working in France. He persuaded the board to buy three so he could evaluate their capabilities and compare them against his own 'Saint' and 'Star' class locomotives. To make the comparisons fairer, he had some of the 4–6–0s converted to 4–4–2 wheel management. No. 102 *La France* was the first to arrive on the Great Western. It was taken into stock in October 1903. Apart from a few modifications made at Swindon, it entered regular passenger service in early February 1904. It was a four-cylinder compound engine. The outside cylinders were high-pressure and drove the rear-coupled axle, while the inside low-pressure drove the leading coupled axle. The large pipes coming from near the dome to the running board supplied the high-pressure steam. No. 102 had French-style nameplates fitted to the cab side. Nos 103 and 104 arrived in 1905. Although they proved to be very capable locomotives, Churchward decided they were no better than his 4–6–0 Simple, so they were withdrawn between 1926 and 1928 and his own locos reverted to 4–6–0s.

GWR 4–4–2 De Glenn no.103 *President* at Paddington, 1906.

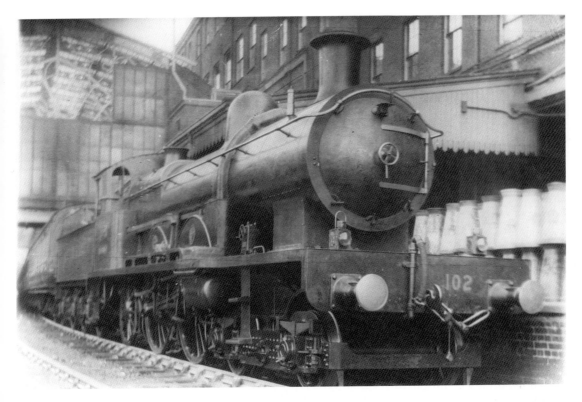

De Glenn 4–4–2 GWR no. 102 *La France* at Paddington, 1906.

GWR 4–4–2 De Glenn no. 104 *Alliance* at Old Oak Common, 1918.

No. 111 *The Great Bear*, Britain's first Pacific locomotive, built as lot 171 in February 1908 at Swindon. As a publicity gimmick it was a brilliant move by the GWR, but its designer George Jackson Churchward did not like the design. As the author of this book, I have seen many photographs of *The Great Bear* and I agree with Churchward's dislike of the engine; it looks like a half-hearted attempt to build a Pacific, without outside steam pipes; the front looks weak and as for the firebox and cab, it all looks like an afterthought. The cab is far too small. His 'Star' class engines built before *The Great Bear* were far more balanced and pleasing to the eye. To me it gives the impression he was persuaded against his will to build it and gave very little thought to its appearance. It was not very successful; it was limited to the Bristol–Paddington line, because of its weight. It was finally decided in January 1924 that it was not worth repairing when it was found the firebox needed major work. It was rebuilt as 'Castle' 4–6–0 although, apart from parts of the frame and the number plates, little else was used. Its eight-wheeled bogie tender, however, lived on and was seen attached to various 'Cities', 'Saints', and 'Stars'. It finished main line service in 1936 and ended its days as a static water tank.

The so-called rebuild of *The Great Bear*, GWR no. 111 *Viscount Churchill* named after the chairman of the GWR who served from 1908 until 1933. With the scrapping of this loco in 1953, all trace of *The Great Bear* had gone, with the exception of the name plates and number plates. This view is of no. 111 at Old Oak Common in 1936.

The 0–4–2T wheel arrangement was popular for branch line working and was to be seen all over the GWR system. Here is no. 1159 standing in Didcot yard on 6 May 1935.

A similar-looking loco, but built a lot later than the previous view. Built in 1932 to Collett's design, GWR no. 4802 is looking good at Swindon in 1935.

A rural setting for this view of GWR no. 5819, an 0–4–2T built in 1933. The station is Pencader which is north of Carmarthen on the Aberystwyth line. Just north of Pencader is the branch to Newcastle Emlyn, which is probably where this train is either heading or coming from. It was photographed in 1933.

Barmouth station is the scene for this picture of GWR 0–4–2T no. 4834, possible station pilot or local stopping passenger train as suggested by the one lamp in front of the chimney. Barmouth station is situated on the edge of the Barmouth Estuary, where the railway crosses the last remaining wood trestle bridge of this size in the country. This type of bridge was common in the early days of railways; however, all but Barmouth were replaced by steel or masonry. The railway is carried on 113 spans of heavy timbers, with two steel girder bridges, one of which swings open for shipping. Many of the timbers have been replaced because of wave action and marine worms.

Barmouth bridge.

GWR 0–4–2T no. 3575 was built in 1876 at Swindon to Dean's design. Ten of these locos were built and all had disappeared by 1948. In the 1930s this loco was shedded at Chester. As this picture is dated 1935, the location may be in the Chester/Birkenhead area.

As has already been stated, the 0–4–2Ts were to be found all over the GWR system. This photograph of GWR no. 565 was taken at Exeter on 7 May 1923.

The 'Armstrong 517' class was built between 1868 and 1885 at Wolverhampton and lasted until the 1940s. The top view is of GWR no. 830, location and date unknown. The lower picture is of GWR no. 574 at Reading in 1934.

GWR 0–4–2T no. 830.

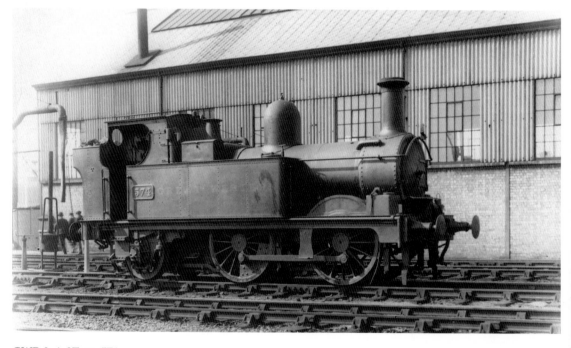

GWR 0–4–2T no. 574.

The 2–4–0T was a wheel arrangement that was very popular in the late 1890s and early 1900s. This photograph is of GWR no. 3596 at Southall on 5 August 1935. It was built in 1899; a cab and bunker were added in 1905, and it was fitted with vacuum trip apparatus for working the Metropolitan lines in the 1920s.

Another 2–4–0T, GWR no. 1497, built 1892. It is seen in about 1908 at an unknown location.

'Metro' tank 2–4–0T GWR no. 3567. It was built in 1894 at Swindon and photographed here in 1933 at Old Oak Common Shed.

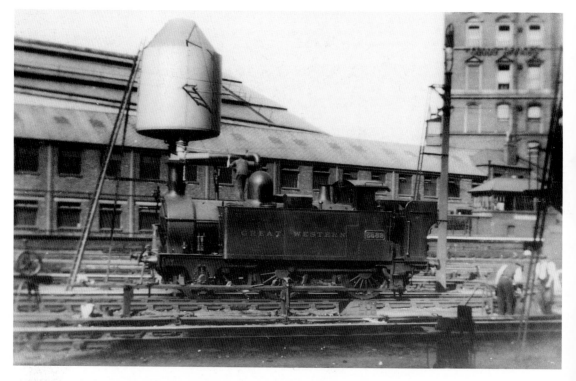

Another 'Metro' tank, this one built a little later than the engine in the view above. It was completed at Swindon in 1899, but photographed a lot later at Paddington, in about 1918. GWR no. 3589 has a little more protection for the crew.

2–4–0T GWR no. 1497, built at Swindon in 1892. This photograph with GWR no. 5806 standing next to it was taken in Bristol St Phillips Marsh in the 1930s.

A Gloucester engine in the 1930s. 2–4–0T GWR no. 3561 is seen at Swindon in 1935.

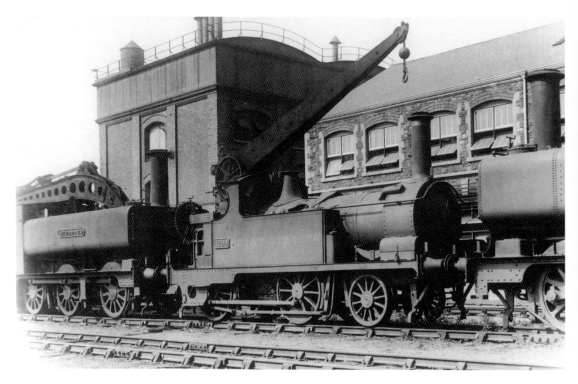

2–4–0T GWR no. 1299 was built in 1878 for the South Devon Railway. Having been taken over by the GWR, it was converted to a crane loco in 1881 and used as a works loco until being withdrawn in the 1930s . It is seen here at Swindon in 1934.

GWR 2–4–0T no. 3586 at Llantrisant in 1930.

GWR 2–4–0T no. 1192 on Exeter Shed in the 1930s.

Another 2–4–0T at rest, GWR no. 3500, this time at Southall in 1935.

Churchward was Dean's assistant at Swindon when the powers within the GWR board encouraged Churchward to design a locomotive especially for working the Bristol–Shrewsbury route through the Severn Tunnel. North of Hereford, the London & North Western Railway (LNWR) was responsible for the upkeep of the track and would not allow 4–6–0 locos to be used. The LNWR were using 4–4–0s northwards from Hereford, and Churchward was determined his engines were superior to Webb's. It had been said that Churchward was influenced by American designs, and his 'Counties' incorporated many American ideas. The first of the 'Counties', no. 3473 *County of Middlesex* was completed at Swindon in May 1904; it had red–brown under frames and a copper-capped chimney. Reputed to be rough riders, they were still well able to cope with the Bristol–Shrewsbury heavy trains.

4–4–0 GWR no. 3801 *County Carlow*. Ten of the 'Counties' were named after Irish counties, especially those working trains going to Fishguard and then by boat to Ireland. No. 3801 was built in 1906 and withdrawn in 1931.

GWR 4–4–0 *County Kilkenny* at Slough in 1912.

GWR no. 3821 *County of Bedford* photographed at Reading 21 July 1923. It was built in 1911 and withdrawn in 1931.

Ranelagh Bridge, Paddington, is the setting for this view of GWR no. 3825 *County of Denbigh* in 1922.

One of the Irish 'Counties' GWR no. 3809 *County of Wexford* at Oxford in 1920. It had been built in 1905, and was scrapped in the early 1930s.

Laira, *c.* 1924. GWR 3812 *County of Cardigan* together with the 'Bulldogs'. They frequently double-headed with 'Kings' over the South Devon banks.

The cleaners on board no. 3479 *County of Warwick* seem far more interested in the photographer than in doing their job. This print was made from a large glass negative, so no doubt the camera would have been a large wood and brass construction and mounted on an equally large tripod. No wonder the cleaners were interested.

GWR 4–4–0 no. 3814 *County of Chester* not in steam on Reading Shed in 1933. They were among the first GWR named engines to be turned out with black cylinders and under frames instead of the Indian red. Built in November 1906 it was taken out of service in June 1933; so perhaps it was awaiting its transfer to Swindon for cutting up!

GWR 4–4–0 'County' no. 3829 *County of Merioneth*, built in 1912, withdrawn in 1932. The last ten of the class which included no. 3829 differed from the other 'Counties' by having curved frames at the front, down to the buffer beam.

Two views of 'Badminton' no. 4107, which was originally no. 3299 *Hubbard*. By 1903 this was changed to *Alexander Hubbard* and renumbered 4107. Built in June 1898, it survived thirty-two years before being withdrawn in February 1930.

No. 4107 at Bristol, 1920s.

No. 4107 at Shrewsbury, 1920s.

It is said that Churchward loved gardening; with a stressful job like locomotive superintendent it was surely a wonderful way to relax, although I think naming a steam engine after flowers is taking it a bit too far (my wife disagrees). Here are two views of the 4–4–0 'Flower' class. The top photograph is GWR no. 4101 *Auricula* taken in 1910, location unknown. The lower is of a double-headed train at Fishguard. With the number of people on the bridge, it would suggest that it is a special train. The lead locomotive is no. 4111 *Anemone* (originally no. 4159), and with it is no. 4116 *Mignonette* (originally no. 4164). Both locos were built in 1908 and withdrawn in 1929.

GWR 4–4–0
no. 4101.

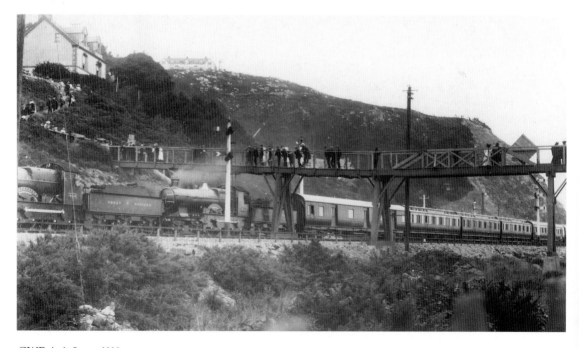

GWR 4–4–0 no. 4111.

The Cambrian Railways were quite extensive in North Wales. The Vale of Rheidol (V of R), which was part of the Cambrian, was taken over by the GWR in 1923. At the Grouping, the three locomotives of the V of R had, however, lost their names. GWR no. 1212 was broken up at Swindon in 1933. The route of the Vale of Rheidol was from Aberystwyth to Devil's Bridge, running through beautiful countryside and, in places, very rugged terrain.

GWR 2–6–2T no. 1212, ex-V of R, awaiting its fate on Swindon dump in 1932.

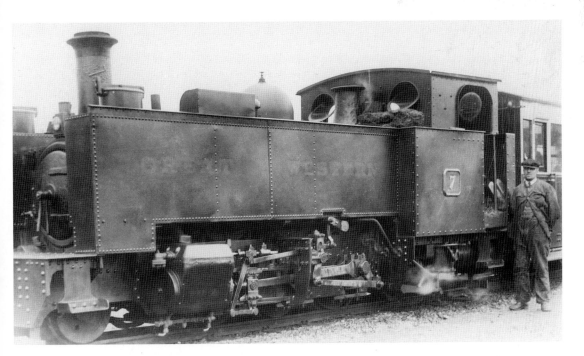

GWR 2–6–2T no. 7, built in 1924 to replace the Vale of Rheidol locos that had been scrapped. This view was taken at Aberystwyth in about 1934.

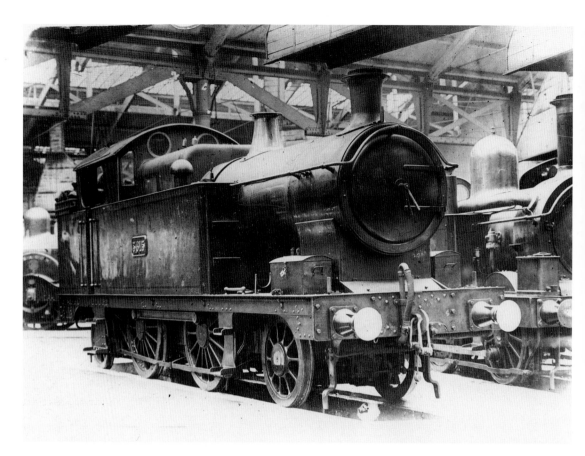

GWR 2–4–2 suburban tank no. 3615, photographed at Old Oak Common in 1908. To the left in the background is 4–2–2 no. 3007 *Dragon*.

Another GWR 2–4–2 tank, no. 3614 with a new boiler and top feed, built in 1902. This photograph was taken at Reading on 21 July 1923.

This view is also at Reading, though a decade later. GWR no. 3610 2–4–2T was station pilot in 1934.

The Midland & South Western Junction Railway went from Cheltenham to Andover, where passengers could then carry on to Southampton. Its loco repair depot was at Cirencester, which opened in 1895. The M&SWJR was absorbed by the GWR at the Grouping in 1923. This photograph is of M&SWJR loco no. 1, designed by James Tyrrell, who was the company's loco superintendent. It was built by the North British Loco Co. in 1905. This view was taken at Swindon in 1932, by which time it was running as GWR no. 1119.

M&SWJR no. 1110 in the scrap line at Swindon.

The '157' class of the GWR consisted of ten engines and each one had slight variations: domes in different positions, cabs slightly different, etc. They were 2–2–2 and were built in 1879 to the standard gauge, and were used principally on the Paddington–Wolverhampton route. This photograph of GWR no. 160 was taken in 1908, location unknown.

Dean 2–6–0 'Aberdare' no. 2670 was built in 1902. It was double-framed, painted Brunswick Green with red under frames and polished brasswork. Its appearance was a little spoilt by having a cast iron chimney instead of the copper-capped one that gave the GWR engines their finished look. This view was taken at Old Oak Common in 1908.

'Aberdare' 2–6–0 no. 2678, in an unknown location. It was built in November 1902 and withdrawn in June 1936.

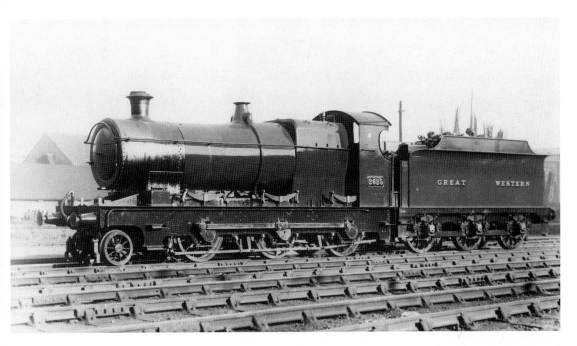

Another green painted, ex-works looking 'Aberdare' at Swindon, *c.* 1932. No. 2625, built in April 1901 and withdrawn in September 1945 had a 4,000-gallon tender, which once belonged to an ROD engine (as in Railway Operating Division, a division of the Royal Engineers), which had been scrapped in 1929.

GWR 2–6–0 'Aberdare' no. 2635 heading a freight train through Oxford in the 1920s. It was reported that during the First World War, 5 million tons of Welsh coal were moved from Aberdare and the Rhondda Valleys to the Royal Navy bases at Scapa Flow and to the south coast harbours. The 2–6–0s were used extensively on these trains, hence their nicknames: 'Aberdares'.

GWR 'Aberdare' 2–6–0 no. 2680 photographed at Hereford. This 'Aberdare' had a long life. It was built in December 1902 and was finally withdrawn in June 1948.

Another 'Aberdare' with a long life, GWR no. 2651, built in 1901. It lasted into British Railways and was taken out of service in June 1949. Photographed at Old Oak Common, its tender piled high with coal and in steam, it will probably head for Acton Yards to take a train of empty coal trucks back to the Welsh Valleys.

The Churchward 2–8–0s were among the most powerful freight locomotives in Britain. On test in 1906, no. 2806 hauled 100 loaded coal trucks from Stoke Gifford to Southall with no trouble at all. It was such a successful design that locomotives of this design were built from 1903 until 1942.

Churchward 2–8–0 GWR no. 2851 built in 1913. This photograph was taken in about 1938, near Ebbw Junction.

GWR 2–8–0 no. 2879 awaiting its next duty at Reading Shed in 1936.

A 2–8–0 was not strictly a GWR engine as it was built by Robinson of the Great Central. A number of them were loaned to the GWR in 1920 and carried the numbers 30xx. They had been requisitioned by the military during the First World War and were commonly known as RODs. Many saw service overseas during the war and, on return to this country, a number were purchased from the government by the GWR. They were all stored in Swindon during 1926, being assessed and repaired at the works if needed. They were given GWR-style number plates and lasted many years.

Another Churchward 2–8–0 GWR no. 4706, photographed on the Sea Front Line at Teignmouth. These 2–8–0s were very efficient and powerful locos. They were originally built for freight train haulage, but they were seen frequently on express passenger trains. Built in 1919 with the standard number one boiler, it was soon found it needed something bigger, so in 1921 the larger number seven boiler was fitted, so the 47s became superb engines. This photograph was taken in 1937.

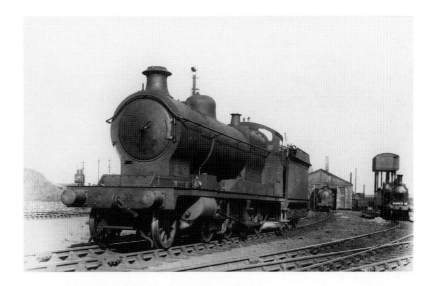

ROD no. 3005 at Reading, 1935.

ROD no. 3014 at Westbury, 1938.

ROD no. 3021 at Reading, 1935.

GWR 'Star' 4–6–0 no. 4060 *Princess Eugenie*, built in 1914 and scrapped in 1952. It is seen here, fitted with a cast iron chimney and all brass beading removed, pulling out of Dawlish station and heading north in 1925.

The GWR 'Saint' class 4–6–0 comprised nearly 100 engines. Several were built experimentally as 4–4–2s but were converted back to 4–6–0s in 1912. They were built in a number of lots between 1902 and 1913. The enginemen referred to them as the 'Twenty-niners'; the enthusiasts were in no doubt they were 'Saints', although there were only twenty out of the ninety-nine named after saints. The rest were ladies, courts, and even names taken from novels. A number of them lasted into British Rail service, the last being withdrawn in 1953.

Photographed at Bristol in 1938 is GWR 4–6–0 no. 2929 *Saint Stephen*, built in 1907 and withdrawn in 1949.

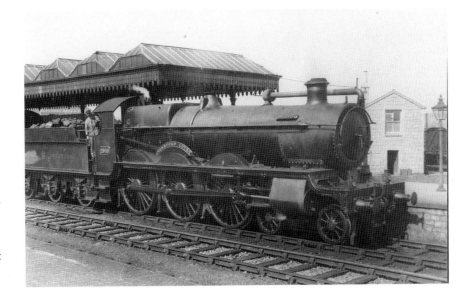

Weston-super-Mare is the setting for this photograph of 4–6–0 no. 2949 *Stanford Court*. Built in 1912, it lasted until 1952.

GWR 4–6–0 no. 2927 *Saint Patrick* in the West Country, posing for the camera at Newton Abbot in the 1930s.

The first of the 'Saint' class named after a court, GWR no. 2931 *Arlington Court* is photographed at Gloucester and seems to have lost the back plate to its nameplate.

GWR 'Saint' 4–6–0 no. 2971 *Albion* at Old Oak Common in 1933. This engine started life as 4–6–0 no. 171 in 1903, but after a few months it was changed to a 4–4–2 on Churchward's instructions, to be used for evaluation against the 4–4–2 De Glenn Compounds. In July 1907, *Albion* became a 4–6–0 again, and for a few months around 1907 it carried the nameplate *The Pirate*, but quickly reverted to the correct name. It met the cutter's torch in 1946.

4–6–0 GWR no. 2928 *Saint Sebastian*, built in 1907 and withdrawn in 1948, arriving in Chester in 1937.

Built in 1905 as a 4–4–2 and numbered 182; a year later it was named *Lalla Rookh*. Here it is leaving Dawlish with a northbound express in 1938, now numbered 2982 and a conventional 4–6–0.

Another Dawlish view, this time southbound. Here is the 1907-built GWR 'Saint' class 4–6–0 no. 2916 *Saint Benedict*, photographed in 1938.

Two GWR 4–6–0 'Saint' class engines that had a long life. Above is no. 2934 *Butleigh Court*, built in 1911 and withdrawn in 1952, photographed heading north out of Dawlish in 1936. Below, ready for its next duty at Swindon in 1935, is no. 2955 *Tortworth Court* built in 1913 and taken out of service in 1950.

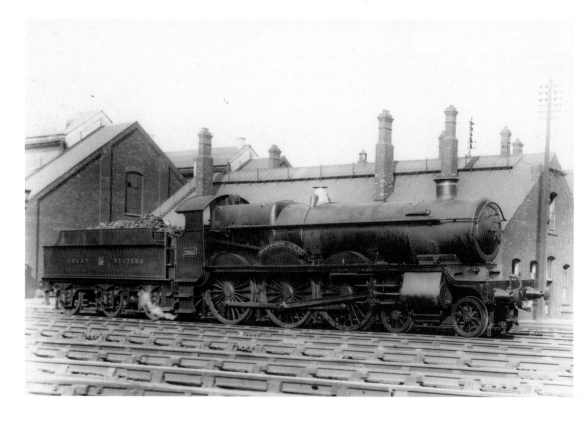

A lady saint in this view at an unknown location; GWR 4–6–0 no. 2918 *Saint Catherine*.

Built in 1906, GWR 'Saint' no. 2902 *Lady of the Lake* works a freight train through Oxford, although it looks like the fireman has forgotten to change the headlamps from express passenger. When this locomotive was new and standing at the head of an express in Paddington, a well-wisher enthusiast presented the driver with a good luck horseshoe. Churchward, on hearing of this gesture, had the horseshoe mounted in the cab of no. 2902 which it carried until its retirement in 1949.

Three views of 'Saints' that were originally 4–4–2s. This view is of GWR no. 2980 *Coeur de Lion* at Dawlish in 1936. When new, it was no. 180.

GWR no. 2981 *Ivanhoe*. Built in 1905 this was another 'Saint' with a long life, not being withdrawn until 1951.

This view taken from the sea wall at Teignmouth is of 'Saint' no. 2986 *Robin Hood*, also built in 1905, originally no. 186.

'Star' 4–6–0 no. 4063 *Bath Abbey*, leaving Dawlish for Plymouth, *c*. 1924. This was another 'Star' that was rebuilt as a 'Castle' in 1937, becoming no. 5083. It survived until 1959.

Armstrong '360' class, built in 1866 as no. 367. It lasted until the early years of the twentieth century, having received many modifications during its lifetime. This photograph is of its final form. The location and date are unknown.

Dean double-framed 0–6–0 GWR no. 2369 at Didcot, 1935. There were twenty of these locomotives weighing nearly 40 tons built between 1885 and 1886. The last of the class was withdrawn in 1946.

The only information about this locomotive that came with the negative was that it was an Armstrong standard 0–6–0, carried the number 44 and that the photograph was taken early in the 1900s.

Ex-Cambrian Railway 0–6–0 built somewhere between 1861 and 1873, carrying GWR no. 908, photographed at Didcot, 16 September 1934.

Built in the 1880s, the 'Dean Goods' had a long and varied life, the last being withdrawn in 1957. A number of this class saw service overseas in both world wars, a large number having been commandeered by the War Department. They were easy locos to drive, very robust, could operate on badly maintained track, and were appreciated by the Railway Operating Corps. Over sixty of these engines were sent to France in 1917. After the war was over they were returned to the GWR and went efficiently about their business until Mr Hitler forced another war on the world. This time, over one hundred of the class were requisitioned for war work, and were put to work in China, Tunisia, Italy, Russia and France. Many were captured and used by the Germans.

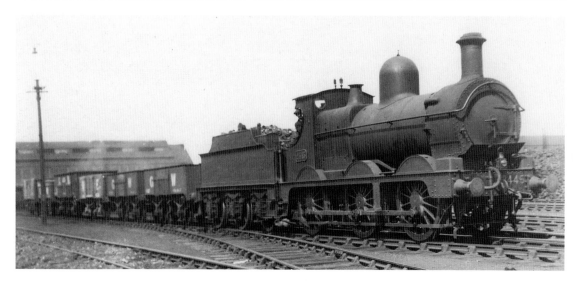

'Dean Goods' built between 1883 and 1899. The last survived until 1957. Photographed at Westbury in 1926, here is GWR no. 2445.

Double-framed 'Dean Goods' 0–6–0 GWR no. 2377 at Exeter.

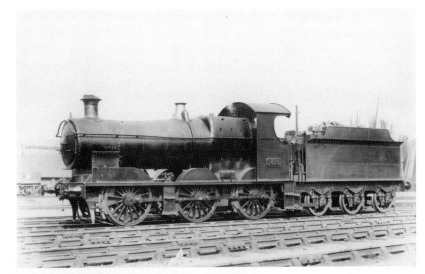

Midland & South Western Junction Railway no. 28, built by Beyer-Peacock in 1902. The M&SWJR was absorbed by the GWR in July 1923, and no. 28 became GWR no. 1013. It is seen here at Swindon in 1930.

Dean 0–6–0 GWR no. 2534 in Swindon running shed in 1937, fitted with a GWR standard snowplough. These snowploughs were fitted to locomotives during the winter months at selected sheds in readiness for heavy snowfalls, so that the snowplough could be clearing the tracks within hours.

Standard 'Dean Goods' GWR no. 2413, photographed at Tyseley in 1935. Its home shed was Stourbridge.

GWR no. 363, built in 1866 to an Armstrong design. Only twelve locomotives were built in this design – the class '360'. The last was withdrawn in 1933. This view in an unknown location is in its final form after a long life.

The Churchward 'Moguls' 2–6–0s numbered 4300, 5300, 6300, 7300 and 9300 were capable of undertaking almost any task they were asked to do and were able to haul heavy freight and express passenger trains at 80mph. Between 1911 and 1932 there were 342 locomotives built. In 1917 a number were sent to France and performed valuable service, a few of the '43xx' class were, during the war years, painted in khaki and green camouflage colours. The '43s' also had the distinction of being the first new engines to have top feed and they were also the last engines to have a Swindon Works plate. A number of modifications were made on the '53xx', and they were renumbered as '83xx', though they gradually reverted to '53xx'. Auto train control was fitted to almost all the 'Moguls' between 1930 and 1932. They were used all over the GWR system, from Cornwall to North Wales and London. The Wolverhampton area alone had ninety engines; Bristol had fifty. Between 1936 and 1939, 100 of the '43xx' and '83xx' were withdrawn, and the wheels and motion were used in the building of the new 'Granges' and 'Manors'.

GWR 2–6–0 no. 6388, built by Robert Stephenson and Co. in 1921. This was the first loco of a batch built outside of the Swindon Works for many years. In 1938 it was shedded at Old Oak Common and, as this photograph was taken in 1937, this suggests the location is the London area.

GWR 2–6–0 no. 5339, built in 1917, withdrawn in November 1960. Here it is photographed at Reading in 1933.

'Mogul' GWR no. 6332, built in 1921, had a good life – it lasted until September 1960. When this photograph was taken in 1936, it was shedded at Birkenhead.

The Midland & South Western Junction Railway ran from Andoversford near Cheltenham and joined the LSWR at Andover, with running rights to Southampton. The route was completed in the 1880s.

GWR no. 1335 was built in the 1890s as M&SWJR no.11. It was photographed at Didcot on 6 May 1935.

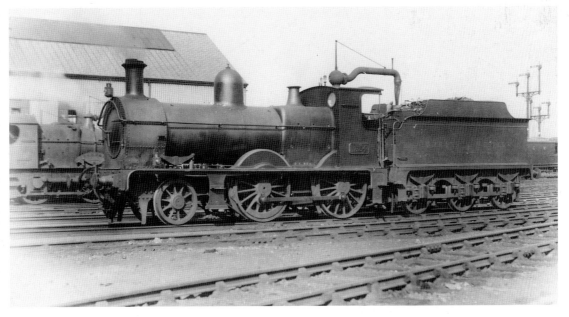

M&SWJR no. 10. Under GWR ownership it became no. 1334 and is seen here in 1933 at Reading.

The two views of the well known 'Barnum' 2–4–0s of the GWR, built in the 1880s. They were used extensively on passenger trains until the larger 4–4–0s came on the scene.

Double framed 'Barnum' no. 3222 at Reading in 1920.

Another Reading view in the 1920s is 'Barnum' 2–4–0 no. 3214.

Armstrong was the designer of these 2–4–0s built in 1873. It was rebuilt in 1885 at Wolverhampton, and known as the 'Bicycle' class (I don't know why). This view of GWR no. 20 is also in Reading.

'Dean' GWR 2–4–0 no. 3245, again at Reading, 1923. Built in 1893, there were twenty in the class and they had all been scrapped by 1930.

Two more views of 'Barnums'.

'Barnum' GWR no. 3215 heading a passenger train at Oxford, *c.* 1920.

This time the location is Swindon in 1933. The loco is GWR no. 3210, another of the 'Barnums'.

GWR no. 1340 *Trojan*, built by the Avonside Engine Co. in 1897. It was based mainly in South Wales, Cathays and Radyr, and then had a period at Oswestry. It also spent time shunting at Park Royal in London. It ended its working life at Alders Paper Mill and was still working there in the 1960s.

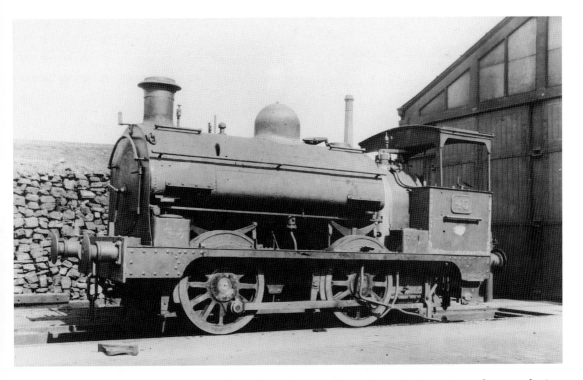

GWR 0–4–0 saddle tank no. 45, originally a Shrewsbury & Birmingham Railway loco, photographed at Wrexham in about 1920.

0–6–0 GWR no. 792, another of the South Wales absorbed companies' engines. This is an ex-Taff Vale, built by Riches Kitson and Co. in 1884, with a steeply sloping boiler, designed especially to work the Pwllyrhebog branch which served the Clydach Vale Colliery. The incline was between 1:13 and 1:29.

0–6–0 GWR no. 1376 working the Weymouth Harbour branch, *c.* 1920.

0–6–2T was a predominant wheel arrangement in the Welsh Valleys – in fact virtually all the locos were of this arrangement when the GWR absorbed the South Wales companies in 1923.

GWR no. 5616 at Ferndale in 1935 with a passenger train heading for the Valleys.

GWR 0–6–2T no. 6612 photographed at Reading, *c.* 1935.

The 'Star' class 4–6–0s of the GWR started with no. 40, which was built as a 4–4–2 in 1906. It did not last very long with this wheel arrangement and was converted to a 4–6–0 and named *North Star*. A further ten 4–6–0s were built in 1907, all receiving names of stars. Further locos were built until the class consisted of seventy-three engines, although none of these were named after stars. There were knights, kings, queens, princes, princesses and even abbeys, but they were all star performers. Designed by Churchward, they set the pattern for main line express engines right up to the early days of British Railways.

GWR no. 4000, *North Star*. This was originally 4-4-2 no. 40 before becoming 4-6-0 no. 4000. It is photographed here in 1933 at Old Oak Common. In 1938 she was a Wolverhampton Stafford Road engine.

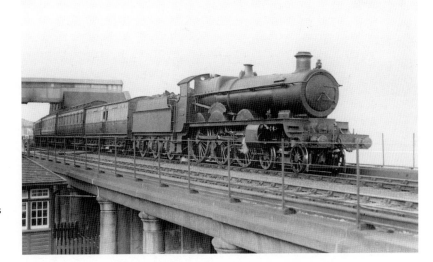

A popular vantage point at Dawlish, 'Star' class no. 4063 *Bath Abbey* heads south out of Dawlish station in 1931 with an elderly rake of coaches.

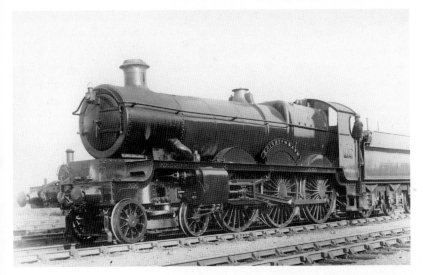

In ex-works condition at Didcot in 1935, is 'Star' 4–6–0 no. 4014 *Knight of the Bath.*

A 1920s view of 'Star' no. 4011 *Knight of the Garter* about to leave Paddington.

Two abbey-named 'Stars' at Shrewsbury. Above is GWR 'Star' class no. 4065 *Evesham Abbey* in 1935, while below is no. 4062 *Malmesbury Abbey* in 1938.

Two more views of 'Stars' at Shrewsbury. Above is GWR no. 4053 *Princess Alexandra* and below we see no. 4043 *Prince Henry*. Both photographs were taken in 1938.

A popular location for railway photography was, and still is, the sea wall at Teignmouth. Here GWR 'Star' no. 4039 *Queen Matilda* is the subject in 1947.

A late evening photograph of GWR 'Star' no. 4008 *Royal Star*, at Old Oak Common in 1936.

Newton Abbot is the location for this photograph of 'Star' no. 4001 *Dog Star* taken in 1918. It has the tall cast iron chimney that rather spoilt its appearance and there was also no lining on the paintwork or polished brasswork.

GWR no. 4009 *Shooting Star* built in 1907. It was rebuilt in 1925 as a 'Castle'. It is seen here at Old Oak Common in 1934.

GWR 'Star' 4–6–0 no. 4015 *Knight of St. John* with a full tender. It was ready to back down to Paddington when this view was taken at Old Oak Common in 1933. Built in 1908, it had a long life and was withdrawn in 1951.

Waiting for the off at Paddington, 'Star' 4–6–0 no. 4038 *Queen Berengaria* is another 'Star' that lasted into British Railways. It is photographed here in 1929. In 1938 it was the only 'Star' shedded at Weymouth.

Seen here in the 1920s at Old Oak Common is another GWR 'Star', no. 4034 *Queen Adelaide*. Built in 1910, it was scrapped in September 1952.

An early view of a 'Star' and a 'County' at Paddington, *c.* 1919. The 'County' is unidentified, but the 'Star' is no. 4007 *Rising Star*.

'Star' no. 4029 *Spanish Monarch* at Newton Abbot in 1931.
When built in 1909, it was named *King Stephen*, but this name was transferred to the new
no. 6029 of the 'King' class in 1930. The engine no. 4029 was withdrawn in 1934.

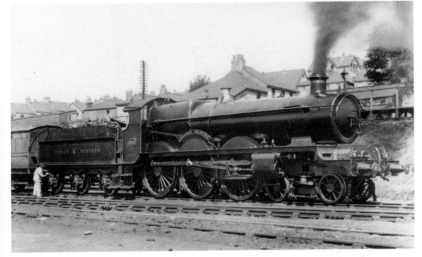

GWR 4–6–0 no. 4042 *Prince Albert* at Laira in 1932. It lasted into British Railways and was withdrawn in 1951.

'Star' 4–6–0 no. 4060 *Princess Eugenie* photographed at Dawlish in 1923. This loco was fitted with an experimental smokebox in the early 1920s. The chimney was moved forward and was a cast iron pattern. It was scrapped in 1952.

4–6–0 GWR 'Star' no. 4001 photographed at Newton Abbot in 1920. Built in February 1907, it was withdrawn in 1934. The first eleven engines of the 'Star' class were named after broad gauge engines of the 1840s. No. 4001 seen here, received the name *Dog Star*. During their early years they were used almost exclusively on the West of England main line. Most of the engines were shedded at Old Oak Common and Plymouth.

A 'Star' at Shrewsbury, no. 4057 *Princess Elizabeth* waiting in the middle road to take a train on to Chester in 1937. Just behind the tender can be seen the front end of an LMS Streamliner running in, after being built at Crewe.

GWR 4–6–0 'Star' no. 4026 *King Richard* waiting for the off at Dawlish in 1924. Its name was changed to *Japanese Monarch* in 1927. This name was not carried for long; it was removed when the Japanese invaded Pearl Harbor during the Second World War.

Teignmouth is the setting for this view of 'Star' no. 4031 *Queen Mary*, built in 1910, scrapped in 1951.

GWR 'Star' no. 4017 *Knight of the Black Eagle* near West Drayton in 1912. It carried this name until 1914 when the First World War started. It was quickly changed to *Knight of Liege*.

Another view at Dawlish. This time we see 4–6–0 'Star' no. 4010 *Western Star*, photographed in the early 1930s.

Backing down into Paddington to pick up its train in May 1935 is 'Star' no. 4071 *Cleeve Abbey*.

Originally GWR 4–6–0 'Saint' no. 2925 *Saint Martin*. When Collett took over from Churchward, he decided to rebuild a 'Saint' with 6ft wheels instead of 6ft 8½in. Various other refinements were made, and in 1924 the first of the 'Hall' class appeared carrying the no. 4900. It retained the name *Saint Martin* until it was scrapped in 1959.

GWR 'Hall' no. 6971 *Athelhampton Hall*, built 1947. Known as the modified 'Halls', no. 6971 was the first of the class to have the new straight-sided tender weighing 49 tons, and holding 7 tons of coal. It was photographed near Plymouth in 1948.

GWR 4–6–0 'Hall' no. 4920 *Dumbleton Hall*, photographed at Old Oak Common in September 1934 with a 3,500-gallon tender.

Another 'Hall' at Old Oak Common ready to back down to Paddington is no. 4928 *Gatacre Hall*.

GWR 4–6–0 'Hall' no. 4947 *Nanhoran Hall* photographed at Reading in 1933. This loco was built in 1929 and spent some time in Cornwall. In 1938 it was shedded at Truro.

Arriving at Newton Abbot with an express bound for the holiday resorts in Cornwall is 'Hall' 4–6–0 no. 4925 *Eynsham Hall*, photographed in 1935.

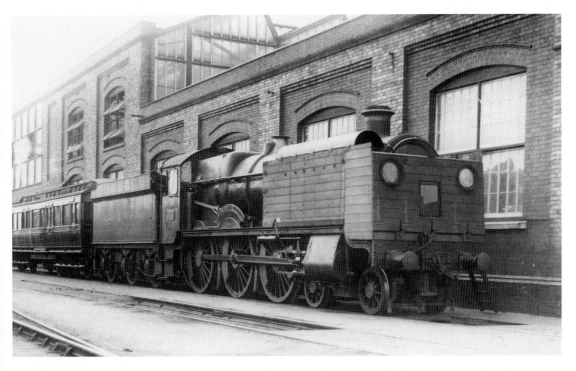

GWR 4–6–0 no. 4930 *Hagley Hall* at Swindon in the 1930s. It has obviously been on test or is going on test. It has the Dynomotor test carriage behind the tender and an indicator shed on the front. It must have been an uncomfortable experience for the two men who rode the engine at speed in such a cramped space trying to read dials and gauges while being bounced around on the buffer beam.

Another experiment on a 'Hall' class, loco no. 4952 *Peplow Hall* photographed at Old Oak Common in August 1934. The cover over the steam pipe conceals an experimental lubricator for use when steam is shut off.

GWR 4–6–0 no. 4931 *Hanbury Hall* at Reading in 1935.

0–8–2T Port Talbot Railway no. 17. On being absorbed by the GWR, it received the number 1358. It was built by Sharpe Stewart in 1901 and was withdrawn in 1948. This photograph is at Danygraig in 1935.

Port Talbot 0–8–2T number 18, GWR no. 1359, built in 1901, withdrawn in 1935, awaiting its fate at Swindon in 1935. The well-known stone carvings of Gooch locos seen above the cab of 1359 are mounted above the main entrance to the GWR offices at Swindon.

These 2–6–2Ts were originally 0–6–0 'Dean Goods' that became redundant. A suburban tank was needed, and with Swindon's ingenuity and the skills of Churchward and his team, the 0–6–0 was transformed into a successful 2–6–2T. This view is of no. 3903 at Tyseley in September 1927. Built in 1898 as an 0–6–0, it carried the number 2501 until rebuilt early in the 1900s. It was withdrawn in 1932.

Another rebuild, GWR no. 3920 photographed in 1928 at Hereford. This loco as an 0–6–0, carried the number 2502. Built in 1898, it was rebuilt early in the 1900s and withdrawn in 1931.

In 1904, Churchward built a prototype 2–6–2T. Numbered 115 it proved to be a winner. It was a small engine, but for its size it was powerful, had very quick acceleration and was just what was needed for steeply graded branch lines. No. 115 was later given the number 4400. A further ten were built, designed at Swindon, but built at Wolverhampton in 1905/6. The number plate was fixed to the side tanks until the 1920s when it was moved to the bunker. Most of the class of ten spent their early life in the West Country until transferred to Shropshire to work local branch lines, including Much Wenlock. This view is of no. 4407 at Newton Abbot in 1924. It was withdrawn in 1953.

Several of these small tank engines were shedded at Plymouth Laira for working the Princetown branch, no doubt carrying many felons to the notorious Dartmoor Prison at Princetown. This view of GWR no. 4408 was taken in Plymouth in the 1920s. Built in 1906, the engine was withdrawn in 1953.

The last engine to be built at Wolverhampton was a fairly large class of 2–6–2T. A bit larger than those featured on the previous two pages, they were capable of hauling passenger trains at 60mph. This view is of no. 3156 photographed at Newton Abbot in May 1923. It has an extended bunker and copper-capped chimney.

GWR no. 4516, also at Newton Abbot, in May 1923. It was built in 1908 and lasted until 1952. A number of the class that lasted until the late 1950s were painted in Brunswick Green and fully lined.

The GWR 'Castles' were designed by Collett, but they were really improved Churchward 'Stars' – not that this takes any of the glory from Collett as he turned a first class 'Star' into a world beating 'Castle'. It is true to say that the 'Castles' influenced design in the other three companies of the Big Four. Stanier left the GWR after rising from apprentice to Collett's assistant, to take charge of loco construction of the LMS at Crewe, and the 'Princess Royals' and many other designs followed. Gresley on the LNER was also influenced by the 'Castles'. At the Empire Exhibition at Wembley in 1925, GWR no. 4073 *Caerphilly Castle* and LNER no. 4472 *Flying Scotsman* stood next to each other. After much arguing about which was the better engine, a trial was organised. No. 4079 *Pendennis Castle* worked from Kings Cross to Doncaster, and *Flying Scotsman* worked Paddington to Plymouth. The GWR won the competition. This picture is no. 4079 *Pendennis Castle* at Old Oak Common in 1934.

Another 'Castle' that took part in an exchange with the LNER was no. 4074 *Caldicot Castle*. Once again it was pitted against *Flying Scotsman* in 1925, and again it proved the winner.

A favourite spot for photographers almost from the start of the railways and photography, were the sea walls at Teignmouth and Dawlish. This view is of GWR no. 5016 *Montgomery Castle* at Teignmouth in the 1930s. The loco was built in July 1932 and was withdrawn in September 1962. In 1938 it was shedded at Penzance.

GWR 'Castle' no. 111 *Viscount Churchill*, a nominal rebuild of Britain's first 4–6–2 Pacific loco, photographed at Old Oak Common in June 1934. The rebuild took to the rails in 1924 and was scrapped in July 1953. Viscount Churchill was Chairman of the GWR.

The driver and fireman of no. 4075 *Cardiff Castle* pause in their oiling of the engine for the cameraman. When finished, they would back down to Paddington for their next duty. This view is at Old Oak Common in May 1934. The loco was built in 1924 and survived until 1963.

Another view of a GWR 4–6–0 'Castle' no. 5013 *Abergavenny Castle* at Old Oak Common, August 1934. Built in 1932, it was withdrawn in July 1962.

GWR 4–6–0 'Castle' no. 5005 *Manorbier Castle*. This was the 'Castle' chosen to be streamlined on orders from the GWR board in 1935. Although Collett did not approve, orders were orders, so, sticking lumps of plasticine on a model paperweight of a 'King' loco, he sent it to the drawing office and told them to get on with it. What came out of the works in 1935 reduced a superb locomotive to something of a caricature. Photographed at Newton Abbot in 1930, 'King' no. 6014 was also treated to the same indignity. It had been built in June 1927 and was withdrawn in February 1960.

GWR no. 5005 *Manorbier Castle* – this is the result of plasticine modelling – photographed at Old Oak Common in September 1935. It was actually worse; there were fairings over the cylinders, but maintenance was almost impossible, so these were removed.

Another popular spot for photographers is the Exe Estuary near Powderham. Here we see GWR 'Castle' no. 5014 *Goodrich Castle* in the 1930s.

In April 1924 Swindon Works received royal visitors when King George V and Queen Mary arrived in the royal train hauled by no. 4082 *Windsor Castle*. They enjoyed a conducted tour of the works, but I am sure the highlight of the visit for King George V was at the end of the visit when he drove no. 4082 from the works to the station, although how he managed it I don't know, as, according to records, apart from the their majesties there were six others on the footplate including the chairman of the GWR and the designer of the 'Castles', C.B. Collett. This view is of no. 4082 *Windsor Castle* at Reading in 1938.

Under the hoist at Laira is GWR no. 5004 *Llanstephan Castle* in 1928 when almost brand new.

Paignton is the setting for this photograph of 4–6–0 'Castle' no. 4099 *Kilgerran Castle*, possibly a holiday express to Bristol or further north. When this photograph was taken in 1938, it was shedded at Exeter. The loco was built in 1926 and withdrawn in September 1962.

GWR 4–6–0 'Castle' class no. 5011 *Tintagel Castle* on Newton Abbot shed in 1934 where it was shedded in the 1930s. It was built in 1927 and withdrawn in 1962.

At an unknown location is no. 4084 *Aberystwyth Castle* in 1928. The black smoke coming from the chimney is very unusual for GWR engines, and quite possibly the fireman was asked to explain. Built in 1925, this engine was withdrawn October 1960.

This location I do know – it's my home station, Bristol Temple Meads, 1934. The engine is no. 5018 *St Mawes Castle* and it is waiting in one of the centre roads ready to relieve another loco on platform seven, which was where expresses from the West of England to Shrewsbury departed from.

One of the longest 'Castle' nameplates, no. 5012 *Berry Pomeroy Castle* in Newton Abbot station, 1936. It is waiting to take over a long-distance express judging by the coal in the tender. Built in July 1927, it was withdrawn in April 1962. In 1938 it was shedded at Cardiff, so perhaps that was where it was going when this photograph was taken.

GWR 4–6–0 'Castle' no. 5046 *Earl Cawdor* at Shrewsbury in 1936. When built in April 1936 it was given the name *Clifford Castle*. It was withdrawn in September 1962.

Named after the engineer-in-chief and the builder of the Great Western Railway, 'Castle' no. 5069 *Isambard Kingdom Brunel* was photographed at its home shed at Old Oak Common in 1947. This 'Castle' does have the longest nameplate, although the original nameplates were not the same radius as the splasher, and looked out of place, so within a few months they had to be changed to the correct style as can be seen in this photograph. It was withdrawn in February 1962.

Another 'Castle' that changed its name was no. 5078 *Beaufort*, originally *Lamphey Castle*. It was changed in January 1941 to honour the aircraft that took part in the Battle of Britain. It received a double chimney in December 1961 and was withdrawn less than a year later. It is photographed at Penzance in 1946.

In the 1920s holiday traffic to the West of England was rapidly increasing. Trains were getting longer and heavier, pushing the 'Castle' class to the limit, so Collett was asked to build a 4–6–0 capable of coping with the heavier loads. As a result the 'Kings' were born. It was also a masterly stroke of publicity as the 'King' class was the most powerful locomotive in Britain, with a tractive effort of 40,000lbs and the GWR was not slow to let the rest of the world know of their success. They were immediately put to work on the Paddington–Plymouth route, hauling the principle expresses including the celebrated 'Cornish Riviera Express'. The first of the class, no. 6000 *King George V* was invited to the USA for the Baltimore & Ohio Railroad Centenary, in which it was given pride of place at the head of the cavalcade.

GWR 'King' 4–6–0 no. 6000 *King George V* at Old Oak Common, August 1934. Built in June 1927, it received a double chimney in 1956.

Last of the class, no. 6029 *King Stephen*, photographed at Teignmouth in 1933. The name was changed to *King Edward VIII* when Edward came to the throne, and was not removed when he abdicated.

GWR 'King' 4–6–0 no. 6014 *King Henry VII* was the second locomotive to be given the horrendous streamlining demanded of Collett by the board of the GWR. Built in May 1928, it received the streamlining in March 1935. As with no. 5005, the skirting round the cylinder area was quickly removed; in fact only six months later in the August of 1935, virtually all the streamlining was removed. By 1943 it was proved it did not enhance performance but made maintenance more difficult. This photograph was taken in 1930 in Paignton. The engine received a double chimney in September 1957, and was withdrawn in September 1962.

'King' no. 6014 seen at Old Oak Common in August 1934, shortly before being sent to Swindon to be streamlined.

'King' no. 6014 *King Henry VII*. This view, again at Old Oak Common, on 28 September 1935 does not look quite as bad as when it emerged from Swindon six months earlier; the tender cowling and the skirting around the cylinders have been removed, as has the bulbous nose. I am sure that were it around now some graffiti artist would have added eyes and a red nose!

GWR 4–6–0 'King' no. 6022 *King Edward III* backing out of Paddington station, making its way back to Old Oak Common in 1935.

This picture is a bit of a mystery to me. It is of GWR no. 6029 *King Stephen*. This name was changed in 1936 so it must have been taken prior to that date. Behind the tender is an LNER engine and a Southern engine is behind the front of no. 6029. They all look in pristine condition, and with two rather official looking gentlemen in bowler hats by the nameplate, it must have been a special event.

Another view at Powderham on the Exe Estuary in Devon. This time no. 6003 *King George IV* has been photographed in 1929. It was built in July 1927, not long before this view was taken.

GWR 4–6–0 'King' no. 6005 *King George II* nearing Birmingham on a two-hour express. It was built in July 1927 and withdrawn in November 1962.

At Newton Abbot in 1929 is the most famous of the class, *King George V* no. 6000, proudly displaying the bell that was presented to it on its visit to the USA. The bell is inscribed, 'Presented to Locomotive King George V by the Baltimore & Ohio Railroad Company in commemoration of its Centenary Celebration Sept 24th–October 15th 1927.' It also carried two medals on the cabside.

GWR no. 6002 *King William IV* on a passenger train at Swindon in 1939; probably on a Bristol–Paddington express.

Another view of no. 6000 *King George V*, this time at Powderham in 1929.

This view is again at Powderham. I can only dream about this location: the sound of the sea, a lovely sunny day, a road right by the side of the railway, a bottle of lemonade, a few sandwiches and then the sound of the 'King' approaching. This time it's no. 6026 *King John*. Such was the day in August 1930.

These 2–8–2Ts were developed from the 2–8–0T, the '52xx' which were successful locos but had a limited distance they could travel because the coal bunker only held about 4 tons. The rebuilds held over 6 tons, and also an extra 700 gallons of water which extended their availability from the South Wales coalfields to Shrewsbury and London. This view is of no. 7205 at Swindon in 1936, rebuilt from no. 5280 in October 1934. Its home shed in 1938 was Aberdare.

GWR 2–8–2T no. 7216, photographed at Severn Tunnel in 1935. It was rebuilt from no. 5291 in November 1934. Next to no. 7216 is 'Bulldog' no. 3305 Tintagel.

The most famous 'City' class 4–4–0 of them all, no. 3717 *City of Truro*, at Shrewsbury in 1929. Built in 1903, its original number was 3440. A year after it was built and nicely run in, it achieved the first recorded 100mph at Whiteball, although this was not announced until many years later, and by then the LNER had claimed that record themselves. On withdrawal it was preserved and went to York Museum in 1931.

Another 'City' 4–4–0 GWR no. 3436 *City of Chester*, photographed at Oxford in 1908. It was renumbered 3713 in later years. The 'Cities' were used on short express working especially on the Oxford, Wolverhampton and London routes and also Bristol to Weymouth and the West Country and South Wales. Built in 1903, no. 3436 was withdrawn December in 1929.

It must have been difficult to tell the difference between the 'Cities' and the 'Flower' class from a distance. There may be detail differences, but the main difference was the nameplates. This photograph is of no. 4154 *Campanula* at Old Oak Common in the 1920s. Its original number was 4106. Built in 1908, it was withdrawn in 1930.

Another 'Flower' GWR 4–4–0 no. 4158 *Petunia* at Leamington in 1926. Originally no. 4110, it was built in 1908 and withdrawn in 1929.

Another 'Flower' at Oxford, GWR no. 4102 *Begonia*, photographed in 1908. The pile of coal in the tender and the driver checking oiling points suggest it is starting its journey from Oxford to London and return. It has enough coal for both ways and it would probably go to Ranelagh Depot just outside Paddington for checking and turning. Built in 1908, it was withdrawn in April 1931.

GWR 'Duke' 4–4–0 no. 3316 *Isle of Guernsey* at Oxford in 1905. A number of the 'Dukes' were altered to 'Bulldogs' between 1906 and 1908, given new boilers and other details, plus extended frames. No. 3316 became 'Bulldog' no. 3312.

'Bulldog' no. 3306 *Armorel*, another rebuilt 'Duke', built as a 'Duke' in 1896 and a 'Bulldog' in 1902. It lasted until 1939.

Known as 'Ringers' because of their oval nameplate and combined number on the cabside, a number of the 'Bulldogs' were so adorned. This view is of no. 3342 *Bonaventura* at Oxford in 1912. Built in 1900, it survived until 1938.

Another 'Ringer', GWR no. 3356 *Sir Stafford* at Reading on 21 August 1923. Its original number was 3368. Also built in 1900, it was withdrawn from service in 1936.

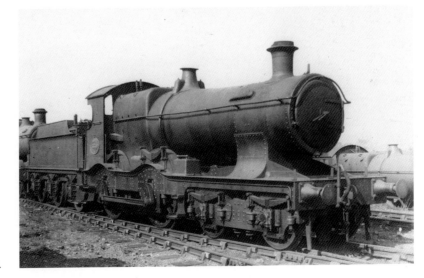

Another 'Bulldog' at Reading – GWR no. 3338 *Swift*, also a 'Ringer'. Its original number when built was 3350 and 1933 was its last year in service.

GWR 'Bulldog' no. 3417. On building in 1906 it received the name *Francis Mildmay*, but in the 1920s Mr Mildmay was made a lord, so in July 1923 the nameplate was changed to *Lord Mildmay of Fleet*. This photograph was taken in 1925 at Bristol. The locomotive had a long life and survived until June 1948. In 1938 its home shed was Banbury.

Another long-surviving 'Bulldog', no. 3430 *Inchcape*, photographed at Barnstaple in 1935. It was eventually withdrawn in 1948.

Built in 1903 4–4–0 'Bulldog' no. 3421 was named *Mac Iver*, but a year or so after building, the name was changed to *David Mac Iver*. Perhaps the gentleman concerned objected to just his surname being used. Photographed here at Oxford in 1906, it was scrapped in 1936.

An unidentified location and date for this view of 4–4–0 'Bulldog', no. 3309 *Maristow*. Built 1907, it was taken out of service in 1934.

Inside the roundhouse at Old Oak Common is 'Bulldog' GWR no. 3407 *Madras*, another long-serving loco. Built in 1904, it was withdrawn 1949.

One of the main duties for 'Bulldogs' in the West Country in the 1920s and '30s was acting as pilot loco on main line expresses between Newton Abbot and Plymouth, to add extra power on the notorious South Devon Banks. Here no. 3398 *Montreal* pilots an unknown 'Hall' on Dainton Bank. It still had a cast iron chimney when this photograph was taken in 1930. It only had a few years to go before being withdrawn after thirty-one years' service in 1935.

Another 'Bulldog' on pilot duty, again on Dainton Bank. GWR no. 3449 *Nightingale* was piloting no. 6016 *King Edward V*. The photograph was taken in August 1937. No doubt carrying many holidaymakers, it was built five years after the photograph [top of Page 142]. It has a number of differences: a copper-capped chimney, deeper frames, enlarged sandboxes, non-fluted coupling rods and various other details. It was withdrawn in 1951.

One of the few unnamed 'Bulldogs', GWR no. 3723 working wrong line. The only information that came with the negative said 'near Slough 1910'. Its number was later changed to 3433 and it survived until 1939. In 1938 its home shed was Oxford.

A side view of GWR 'Bulldog' no. 3321 *Brasenose*, one of the 'Ringers' at Paddington, 1921. The nameplate also incorporates a shield of the GWR coat of arms. Built in 1899, it was scrapped in 1935.

The original Paddington station was opened in 1838. It was a temporary wooden structure with offices located in the arches of Bishop Road Bridge. The Paddington on today's site was opened in 1854. In the nineteenth century the village of Paddington was a mile from London. The station – three bays with an arched roof – was of course designed by Brunel, assisted by Sir Matthew Digby Wyatt. An additional bay was added in 1916. Various improvements have been made over the years and the last major work was in the 1930s when the frontage was modernised. The Great Western Hotel, which is part of the station, has 165 rooms and when built was the largest in the country. The concourse, the large area where passengers gather to buy food and drink from the refreshment rooms, purchase a magazine or paper to read on their journey, or to look at the destination indicator was known as 'The Lawn'. In the early days of the station, this area was an untidy collecting place for barrows, horse-drawn carts and was probably full of weeds – hence why it was jokingly called 'The Lawn' by railway employees. The name stuck. There was also a royal waiting room for Queen Victoria's use. The queen made her first railway journey on 13 June 1842 from the original Paddington station. She must have enjoyed the experience for she went on to make many more journeys in her long reign. The broad gauge finally gave way to the standard gauge, 4ft 8½in in May 1892, when the last 7ft gauge train, the 5 p.m. 'West of England Express' headed by 4–2–2 *Bulkeley* left Paddington. Once this train had finished its journey, the massive job of converting from broad gauge to standard gauge was started. Much preparatory work had taken place, bringing all 7ft gauge stock back to holding sidings in Swindon. Track had been prepared and the services of thousands men were organised. It was like a military operation and within a couple of days the broad gauge was no more.

GWR 'Bulldog' no. 3386 *Paddington*, photographed at Reading in 1923. This engine was used as station pilot at Paddington in the early days. Built in 1903, it lasted until 1949.

'Bulldogs' at opposite ends of the GWR empire: no. 3405 *Empire of India* approaching Shrewsbury station in 1933 . . .

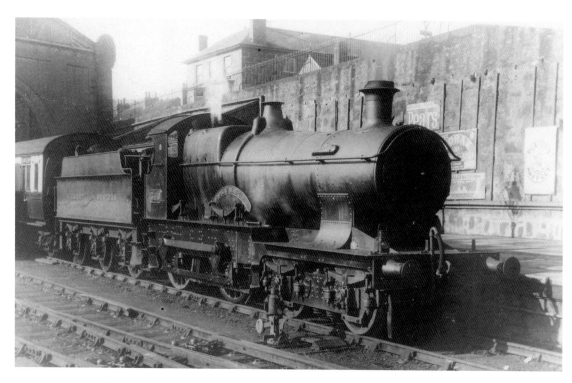

. . . and at the furthest point west, GWR 'Bulldog' no. 3410 *Columbia* at Penzance in 1921.

Named after its place of birth is 'Bulldog' no. 3384 *Swindon*, although when taking to the main line on leaving the works it carried the name *Liverpool* for some obscure reason. Built in 1903, it was withdrawn in 1936. The nameplate was changed within a couple of months. It is photographed at Ranelagh Depot, Paddington, in 1925.

The location of this photograph is easy to identify, as Newton Abbot seems to take pride in stacking large lumps of coal like this. The photograph is of 'Bulldog' no. 3357 *Trelawney* in 1924.

'Bulldog' no. 3401
Vancouver at Swindon on 11
September 1935.
Built in 1904, it was taken
out of service in 1949.

GWR 'Bulldog' no. 3425 at
Swindon in June 1935.
This was one of the
unnamed ones. Its original
number when built was
3715. Built in 1906, it was
scrapped in 1938.

GWR 'Bulldog' no. 3449
Nightingale looks as
though it is ex-works,
photographed in 1935.

It is difficult to tell the difference between the 'Atbaras' and the 'Bulldogs', the main difference being wheel size. The 'Bulldogs' wheels are 5ft 8in, the Atbaras 6ft 8½in, which of course would be the size of the future 'Castles'.

'Atbara' GWR no. 4120 *Atbara* photographed at Leamington in 1920. This loco was temporarily named *Royal Sovereign* for Queen Victoria's funeral train.

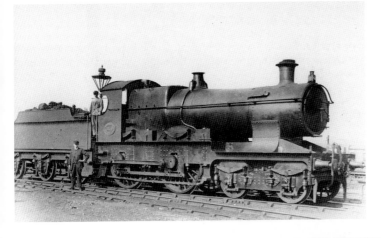

An 'Atbara' at Bristol, GWR no. 4130 *Omdurman* in 1921. Built in 1900 and withdrawn in 1930, its original number was 3384.

Built in 1901 as 'Atbara' GWR no. 3405 *Mauritius*, a year later it was rebuilt with a larger boiler and detail differences, and became the first of the 'City' class. Photographed at Ranelagh Depot, Paddington, in 1922, it was withdrawn in 1928.

Two early views of 'Atbaras', the first is of GWR no. 3412 *Singapore* built in October 1901. The photograph was taken in 1904 but no location was given; frustratingly the first word on the signal cabin in the background is obscured.

Second is this early view of GWR no. 4129 *Kekewich* on an express in about 1908, having been built in 1900. It last saw service in 1928.

'Atbara' no. 3375 *Baden Powell* can be seen receiving a squirt from the oiling can at Oxford in 1908. It changed its name several times in its early life, becoming *Pretoria* for a city imperial volunteer special on 29 October 1900. It changed again in 1902 to *Britannia* for working royal trains. Late in 1902 it became *Kitchener* for a special train. Built in 1900, it was taken out of service in 1928.

The GWR invested in early diesel railcars for working branch lines. They were quite streamlined and cost-effective, and were very popular with the villagers that the branch lines served. The first built were very successful and in a short while of them first entering service, more powerful engines were installed and the railcars were working longer routes.

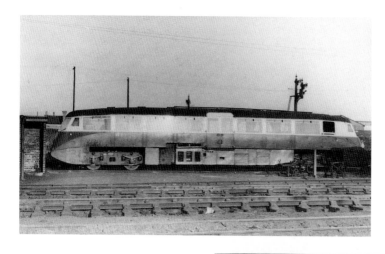

W1, the first railcar built, entered service in 1934 with a 121bhp engine. It could carry sixty-nine passengers.

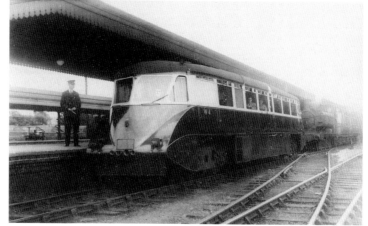

W4 with a larger 242bhp engine. It also had a toilet and buffet service. It is photographed here at Princes Risborough.

W5 at an unknown location.

W20, built in 1940, collecting passengers in Shrewsbury's main line station.

W29 entering Reading station.

W33 hauling a single carriage, also photographed at Reading.

Branch line stations have always been fascinating with their often unhurried way of life, porters who were helpful and if the train were a little late, it did not matter.

A pretty little branch line terminus, but with no information, although it has an air of the 1930s.

'Chard G.W.' – again very few details.

The signal-box and overbridge at Williton, opened in 1862 by the Bristol & Exeter Railway.

Bala Lake Halt on the GWR
Mid Wales line.

Wells Priory Road in the
1930s.

Brimscombe, near Stroud in
the Cotswolds.

Crowcombe station on the Taunton–Minehead branch line.

Exeter St David's station photographed just before nationalisation in 1947.

Kingswear could be called a branch line, but it received trains from all over the country, many headed by 'Kings' and 'Castles' direct from London. There are extensive carriage sidings and a turntable to the right of the photograph. Apart from summer holiday visitors, the Royal Navy training college for officers was the other side of the river at Dartmouth.

Aynho Junction: where the London–Birmingham line joins the Didcot–Birmingham line just before Banbury.

Pangbourne on the fast stretch of Brunel's line between Reading and Didcot.

Builth Road low-level on the Craven Arms–Swansea line.

Pembrey and Burry Port, opened in 1852 on the direct route to Fishguard Harbour for the Irish mails and passenger ships that used the dock.

As the last picture in this book, I have chosen a personal favourite – Chipping Norton station. On the edge of the Cotswolds, it has a lovely setting, peaceful and relaxing, where you could sit for hours enjoying a drink and a sandwich, and taking an occasional photograph of a train passing through the station. I will stop now and have a cup of tea. I hope you have enjoyed a dip back in GWR days, as I have in selecting these photographs from my extensive archive of negatives.